7/08

CHESTER A. ARTHUR
OUR TWENTY-FIRST PRESIDENT

by Carol Brunelli

THE CHILD'S WORLD®

PUBLISHED IN THE UNITED STATES OF AMERICA

THE CHILD'S WORLD®
1980 Lookout Drive • Mankato, MN 56003-1705
800-599-READ • www.childsworld.com

ACKNOWLEDGMENTS
The Child's World®: Mary Berendes, Publishing Director

Creative Spark: Mary McGavic, Project Director; Melissa McDaniel, Editorial
Director; Deborah Goodsite, Photo Research

The Design Lab: Kathleen Petelinsek, Design; Gregory Lindholm, Page Production

Content Adviser: David R. Smith, Adjunct Assistant Professor of History,
University of Michigan–Ann Arbor

PHOTOS
Cover and page 3: National Portrait Gallery, Smithsonian Institution/Art Resource,
NY (detail); National Portrait Gallery, Smithsonian Institution/Art Resource, NY

Interior: The Art Archive: 7 (The Harry T. Peters Collection/Museum of the City
of New York/57.300.519), 16, 22, 24 and 39, 37 (Culver Pictures); Corbis: 9
(Oscar White), 10, 33 (Corbis), 13 (C. O. Bostwick/Medford Historical Society
Collection), 17, 18 (Bettmann); The Granger Collection, New York: 20, 29; Getty
Images: 32 (Kean Collection); iStockphoto: 44 (Tim Fan); Library of Congress: 4,
8, 12, 15, 19, 21, 25, 35; North Wind Picture Archives: 31 (North Wind); Picture
History: 11; U.S. Air Force photo: 45; U.S. Naval Historical Center: 34; Vermont
Division for Historic Preservation, President Chester A. Arthur State Historic Site:
5 and 38; White House Historical Association: 26 (Francis Benjamin Johnston
Collection), 28, 30 (detail), 36 (detail) and 39 (White House Collection); XNR
Productions: 23.

LIBRARY OF CONGRESS CATALOGING-IN-PUBLICATION DATA
Brunelli, Carol.
  Chester A. Arthur / by Carol Brunelli.
    p. cm. — (Presidents of the U.S.A.)
  Includes bibliographical references and index.
  ISBN 978–1–60253–050–8 (library bound : alk. paper)
  1. Arthur, Chester Alan, 1829–1886—Juvenile literature. 2. Presidents—United
States—Biography—Juvenile literature. I. Title. II. Series.

  E692.B775 2008
  973.8'4092—dc22
  [B]
                                    2008000523

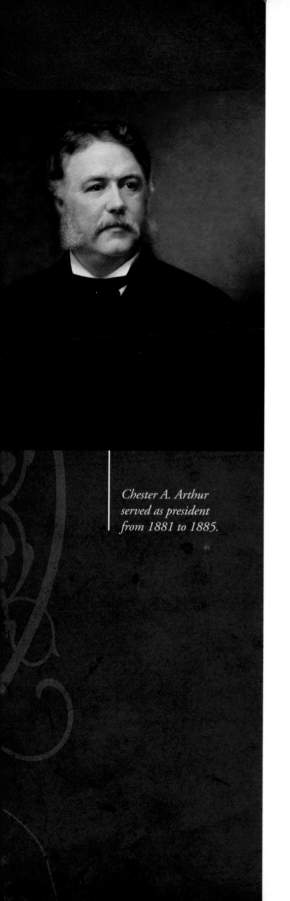

Chester A. Arthur served as president from 1881 to 1885.

TABLE OF CONTENTS

chapter one
ABOLITIONIST AND LAWYER   4

chapter two
POLITICAL LEADER OF NEW YORK CITY   10

chapter three
AN HONEST PRESIDENT   20

chapter four
A MAN TO RESPECT   32

Time Line   38

Glossary   40

The United States Government   42

Choosing the President   43

The White House   44

Presidential Perks   45

Facts   46

For More Information   47

Index   48

ABOLITIONIST
AND LAWYER

The fifth child and first son of an Irish American minister brought great happiness to a humble farmhouse in North Fairfield, Vermont. This boy, Chester Alan Arthur, who was born on October 5, 1829, was one of nine children. He would grow up to surprise his family, friends, and foes by becoming the 21st president of the United States.

Arthur's father, William, came from Ireland. He moved to Canada as a young man and began working as a schoolteacher in a village near the Vermont border. He soon met 18-year-old Malvina Stone, whose family came from Vermont and New Hampshire. In 1821, the young couple married.

William Arthur was born in the village of Cullybackey, in what is now Northern Ireland.

During the next few years, the Arthur family lived in many Vermont towns, where William taught school, studied law, and finally became a minister. The family settled in New York State in 1835. That year, William Arthur helped start the New York Anti-Slavery Society.

Chester Arthur spent his early years in this tiny cabin in North Fairfield, Vermont.

Both William and Malvina were deeply religious. They had strong feelings about what was right and wrong. They believed that all human beings were created equal and that all people deserved to be treated with respect. Because of this, they fought to end slavery in the United States. At the time, Americans who wanted to end, or abolish, slavery were called abolitionists.

The Arthurs moved to Saratoga County, in western New York, in 1839. William Arthur continued working as a minister. This gave him a chance to share his antislavery beliefs with the people who came to his services. Young Chester grew up hating slavery. He held many of his parents' strong opinions. After he became interested in **politics,** he would have the chance to share his beliefs with others.

By 1845, Chester was ready to attend college, so he enrolled at Union College in Schenectady, New York. He was a friendly and outgoing young man, who

Chester Arthur often told people that his birth year was 1830, but he was actually born in 1829.

wrote for the school newspaper and was a member the **debate** club.

Chester Arthur was tall, social, and good-looking. At Union College, he shed his drab style and humble beginnings. He developed a taste for high fashion and was careful about his clothes. He also grew a mustache and long sideburns called "muttonchops."

Arthur graduated in 1848 and decided to study law. To help pay for his studies, he worked as a schoolteacher. In 1851, he became the principal of a school that met in the basement of his father's church in North Pownal, Vermont.

Arthur moved to New York City in 1853 and began working for Erastus D. Culver, a friend of his father. Culver had been an outspoken antislavery congressman from New York State. Tensions were rising between northerners and southerners over the issue of slavery. Many northerners wanted to stop the spread of slavery into the new **territories.** But some people in southern states were afraid that if slavery did not expand as the nation expanded, it might eventually be abolished. They did not think they could run their large farms if slavery were abolished.

In 1854, Arthur attended a meeting called the Anti-Nebraska **Convention** in Saratoga Springs, New York. The purpose of the meeting was to protest the Kansas-Nebraska Act. This act allowed the white settlers of Kansas and Nebraska to decide for themselves whether to allow slavery in their territories. This raised the possibility that new slave states would enter the **Union.**

To friends and family, Chester Arthur was known as "Chet."

More than 100 graduates of Union College have become members of Congress.

Many abolitionists—including Chester Arthur—were furious. At the Anti-Nebraska Convention, people joined together to form the Republican Party of New York State. This new **political party** was started in part to fight the spread of slavery into new territories.

That same year, Arthur passed his law exams. He went to New York City to work in Erastus Culver's firm and quickly became known as a supporter of **civil rights** for African Americans. First, Arthur helped defend Elizabeth Jennings, an African American schoolteacher who was forced off a streetcar that was reserved solely for white people. Arthur won $250 for Jennings in a lawsuit, which was a lot of money at the time. Because of this case, African Americans were guaranteed the right to ride on any streetcar in New York City. Due to his success in trying civil rights cases, Chester Arthur

When Arthur moved to New York, more than half a million people lived there.

In the early 1850s, Arthur was the principal of a school in North Pownal, Vermont. Another future president, James Garfield, later taught penmanship there. Garfield was elected president in 1880, and Arthur was his vice president.

became a partner in Culver's law office, and the name changed to Culver, Parker & Arthur.

Arthur worked with Culver to win another civil rights case. A man named Jonathan Lemmon had brought eight enslaved African Americans with him from the southern state of Virginia to New York. Slavery was legal in Virginia, but it was illegal in New York. The African Americans wanted their freedom. Arthur and Culver fought for them in court. Judge Elijah Paine of New York ruled in favor of the enslaved people, saying that because they had come to a free state, they were now free.

The Lemmon case made Arthur famous in New York City. In 1856, he opened his own law office. He also worked for the **campaign** of John C. Frémont, the Republican **candidate** for president. From that time forward, Arthur was an active member of the Republican Party.

Arthur became a leading lawyer in New York in the 1850s. He made a name for himself working on cases that helped African Americans gain their rights.

THE REPUBLICAN PARTY

Today's Republican Party was formed during the 1850s. At the time, the issue of slavery was threatening to divide the nation. The two most powerful political parties, the Whigs and the Democrats, were divided on the issue as well. The Whigs wanted to abolish slavery. Democrats wanted to protect it. Some people were not satisfied with either political party. They began talking about forming a new one.

Alan Earl Bovay was one of the founders of the Republican Party. He believed the new party should fight slavery and represent other interests of the northern states. He called the party "Republican" because the word describes a place where all citizens have equal rights. Years before, Thomas Jefferson had chosen "Republican" to refer to his party, the Democratic-Republican Party. Later, that party became known simply as the Democratic Party.

In 1854, Chester Arthur and others at the Anti-Nebraska Convention in Saratoga Springs, New York, created the New York Republican Party. It was committed to preventing slavery from expanding into the territories.

In 1856, Arthur worked on the campaign of John Frémont, the first Republican presidential candidate. Although the Republicans lost the election to the Democrats, it won a third of the total vote. By 1860, the Republican Party had gained strength. Its candidate, Abraham Lincoln (above), won the election that year, making him the first Republican president.

POLITICAL LEADER OF NEW YORK CITY

After leaving Culver, Parker & Arthur, Chester Arthur's career and reputation grew. He formed a business partnership with his friend Henry D. Gardiner. As partners, Arthur and Gardiner wanted to expand their law offices in the American West. They decided to visit Kansas. At the time, Kansas was known as "Bleeding Kansas" because people there were in a violent fight over slavery and the Kansas-Nebraska Act. Because of the unrest, Arthur and Gardiner quickly gave up their plans and returned to New York City.

Waiting for Arthur in New York was a lovely young woman named Ellen Lewis Herndon. Ellen, known as "Nell" to her family and friends, was a cousin of one of Arthur's friends. Her father was a naval officer from a well-to-do Virginia family. Nell and Chester had met in 1856 and had

Ellen Arthur, in a photograph taken around 1865

quickly fallen in love. They were married in October 1859. Nell had many social connections that helped make Chester more comfortable among the city's wealthy. Soon, the Arthurs were popular guests and hosts of lavish parties.

Though Nell was a southerner whose family owned slaves and Arthur was a passionate abolitionist, they were nonetheless devoted to each other. Their first son was born in 1860. He died just two years later, leaving his parents heartbroken. The couple later had a son, Chester Jr., and a daughter, Ellen.

Chester Arthur (left) poses with two of his brothers-in-law. This photograph was taken in 1856, the year he met Ellen Herndon.

During the first two years of the American Civil War, Arthur was the quartermaster general of New York State. He was in charge of organizing food and supplies for U.S. soldiers.

Life during the Civil War was difficult for Chester and Nell Arthur. Dabney Herndon, the cousin who had introduced them, was a Confederate soldier and prisoner of the Union army. Chester was against slavery, but to honor his wife, he had the cousin freed.

In 1860, Arthur campaigned in New York City for the Republican presidential candidate, Abraham Lincoln. Arthur also worked hard for the reelection of Edwin D. Morgan, the governor of New York.

Tensions between the North and South continued to grow. Many Southerners feared that Abraham Lincoln would abolish slavery. After he was elected president in November 1860, Southern states began seceding from, or leaving, the Union. They organized themselves into a new nation they called the Confederate States of America. It was also known as the Confederacy. President Lincoln did not believe that the Southern states had the right to secede. He would fight to keep the Union whole.

The Civil War began in 1861. Lincoln put Governor Morgan in charge of New York's volunteer soldiers. Morgan named Chester Arthur inspector general and then **quartermaster** general of the New York Volunteers.

At the start of the Civil War, many people in the North believed the Union army would quickly overcome the Confederate army. But the Southern states were determined. As the conflict grew, the Union army needed more soldiers. President Lincoln asked New York State to provide 30,000 troops for the cause. It was up to Arthur to ensure that these men had the food, shelter, uniforms, and weapons they needed to go into battle. In 1862, President Lincoln requested 120,000 more soldiers from New York State. Winter had arrived, making Arthur's responsibility of supplying the soldiers with food and warm clothes all the more difficult. Arthur rose to the task. Many important politicians took notice, admiring his management skills. Years later, Arthur's son declared that the time

As wealthy New Yorkers, the Arthurs enjoyed a privileged life. They lived in an elegant home filled with fine furniture and had many servants. Their children did not attend school. Instead, they took their lessons from private tutors who taught them at home.

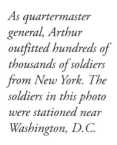

After leaving the post of quartermaster general, Arthur rightfully kept the title "General."

when Arthur was quartermaster general were some of the finest years of his father's life.

In 1863, a Democrat named Horatio Seymour was elected governor of New York. He **appointed** a Democratic quartermaster general, so Arthur returned to his law practice. But he stayed in close contact with the city's Republican Party. The boss, or leader, of the party in New York was Senator Roscoe Conkling. Arthur supported Conkling and became one of his most important assistants.

Conkling and his followers were called Stalwarts. The Stalwarts were a small **faction** within the Republican Party, and they did not always agree with other people in the party. In 1868, the Stalwarts supported General Ulysses S. Grant as the Republican candidate for president, and he won the election.

As quartermaster general, Arthur outfitted hundreds of thousands of soldiers from New York. The soldiers in this photo were stationed near Washington, D.C.

President Grant wanted to reward the people who had helped him win the election. This included Arthur, who was a loyal Stalwart Republican. In 1871, Grant appointed Arthur to a powerful position, the collector of the Port of New York. He was now in charge of the New York **Customs** House.

The customs collector was an important political position. Arthur oversaw the movement of all goods into busy New York Harbor. He collected taxes charged on all items brought from other countries to sell in the United States. The position was so powerful that Arthur became the leader of the Republican Party in New York City. He was also the chairman of the Republican state committee.

The New York Customs House was the largest government office in the nation, with more than 1,000 employees. As the collector of the Port of New York, Arthur was in charge of its operations.

Arthur used his new power to make the Republican Party stronger. He gave jobs to many members of the party. In fact, he gave Senator Conkling's followers, the Stalwarts, many positions at the customs house. Although Arthur was an honest man, he gave too many jobs to the Stalwarts. These people worked hard for the election of Republicans, but they did not work very hard at the customs house. Some people were angry that these men were paid to help the Republican Party, not to do their jobs.

In 1877, Rutherford B. Hayes became president. Hayes was a Republican, but he did not like the Stalwarts. He later fired Arthur from the position of collector of the Port of New York. President Hayes said Arthur had used the government's money to reward

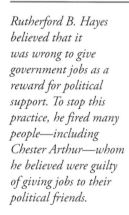

Chester Arthur earned about $50,000 a year as collector of the Port of New York. At the time, an average worker earned about $500 a year.

Rutherford B. Hayes believed that it was wrong to give government jobs as a reward for political support. To stop this practice, he fired many people—including Chester Arthur—whom he believed were guilty of giving jobs to their political friends.

Roscoe Conkling was the leader of the Stalwarts. He gained power by passing out jobs to his supporters. Arthur was one of his top assistants.

his political supporters. Arthur did have connections with many of the powerful New York politicians of the time, but no one ever proved that he had done something wrong. Hayes soon hired one of his own supporters as the collector of the Port of New York. Some Americans thought Hayes had treated Arthur unfairly. Many Republicans still supported Arthur.

In 1880, it was time for the Republicans to choose a candidate for the next presidential election. At first, they could not make a decision. After some time, they made a **compromise.** They **nominated** James Garfield of Ohio as their candidate for president. They chose Arthur as their candidate for vice president. He was an important figure in New York, and they hoped he would win votes for the party. Senator Conkling did

While Arthur was the collector of the Port of New York, people called him "the Gentleman Boss." He was called "Gentleman" because he wore fine clothing, had good manners, loved elegant parties and good food, lived in a beautiful home, and liked to talk about books and other intellectual things. He was called "Boss" because he was a powerful member of his political party.

17

Republicans gathered in Chicago for their national convention in 1880. They selected James A. Garfield as their presidential candidate and Chester A. Arthur as their vice-presidential candidate.

After Arthur's wife died in 1880, he placed a vase of roses by her portrait every day.

not like James Garfield. In fact, he told Arthur to turn down the nomination, saying, "Drop it as you would a red hot shoe from the forge." Arthur refused. "The office of the vice president is a greater honor than I ever dreamed of attaining," he said.

Despite the nomination, 1880 was not a happy year for Arthur. That year, his wife caught a cold that turned into **pneumonia.** Arthur was out of town when he heard of her illness. He caught a train immediately, but by the time he reached Nell, she was no longer aware of her surroundings. He stayed by her bedside for 24 hours, hoping she would wake. She did not. She died the next day at the age of 42. Deeply saddened, Arthur felt guilty for having spent so much time away from home, pursuing his career and relaxing with his friends. "Honors to me," he said, "are not what they once were."

PATRONAGE AND THE STALWARTS

Patronage is the act of giving people government jobs in exchange for their loyalty to a party. Party leaders worked hard to get good jobs for their friends and supporters. This practice often allowed people who were not qualified to hold positions of responsibility that paid excellent wages. Other people who might do the job better, but who had differing views, were out of luck. In exchange for a job, some people were even forced to give part of their wages to the political party. As chairman of the New York State Republican Committee, Chester Arthur charged government employees 3 percent of their annual **salary.**

The Stalwarts' power was based on the patronage system. Although both President Rutherford B. Hayes and the Stalwarts were Republicans, Hayes did not like the Stalwarts. One reason was that Hayes was against the patronage system. Hayes instead wanted to create a "merit system," which would give jobs to people who were qualified, not to the friends of politicians.

Chester Arthur was a Stalwart. When President Hayes fired him from his position as collector of the Port of New York, Arthur worried it might hurt his political career. But the Stalwarts still supported him, and his career continued. In fact, just two years later, the Republicans selected Arthur as their vice presidential candidate. The cartoon below shows president Hayes kicking Arthur out of the New York Customs House.

ANOTHER PRESIDENT WHO HAD A RISE IN THE WORLD.

AN HONEST PRESIDENT

Garfield and Arthur had their work cut out for them in the election of 1880. The Republicans had been the party that had won the Civil War, but after the war, the Democrats had become a strong political force. They argued that the **federal** government, which was controlled by the Republican Party, was not doing enough to help the former Confederate states. They also called the Republicans corrupt.

Until this time, presidential and vice presidential candidates generally remained in the background during an election. But James Garfield wanted to talk to the people directly. He conducted his campaign from the front porch of his house in Ohio. Arthur, in the meantime, went to work seeking campaign funds and support from powerful New Yorkers. Their strategy worked, and the two were sworn into office in March 1881.

Chester A. Arthur in 1881

THIS IS NOT THE NEW YORK STOCK EXCHANGE, IT IS THE PATRONAGE EXCHANGE, CALLED U. S. SENATE.

After the election, the question of patronage became a problem. Conkling wanted President Garfield to find jobs for loyal Republicans in New York State, especially for Stalwarts. He also wanted the president to ask his advice about who should get these jobs. Arthur agreed with Conkling, who had always supported him in the past. At first, Garfield tried to reach a compromise and give Conkling part of what he wanted. But Conkling wanted all or nothing. He believed every position should go to Republican Stalwarts. The president refused to go along with him. Finally, Conkling

In the 1880s, many Americans believed politicians cared more about passing out patronage jobs than they did about governing. This cartoon depicts politicians making patronage deals on the floor of the U.S. Senate. Arthur is shown at the left receiving orders for jobs.

Garfield was the second president to be killed in office. The first was Abraham Lincoln.

When Chester Arthur was sworn in as president, he became the third person to serve as president within a single year. Rutherford B. Hayes left office in March 1881 (when Garfield was sworn in). Arthur became president after Garfield's death six months later.

resigned his seat in the Senate in protest. People respected Garfield for standing up to the powerful Stalwarts, but he had made enemies as well.

On July 2, 1881, soon after Conkling left the Senate, a mentally ill man named Charles J. Guiteau shot President Garfield. As Guiteau fired the gun, he declared, "I did it and will go to jail for it. I am a Stalwart of the Stalwarts, and Arthur is president now." Some people took this to mean that Arthur had something to do with the shooting. It was soon proven that this was not the case. But Arthur was hurt by such terrible words and by suggestions that he take over the presidency while Garfield was still alive. "I am overwhelmed with grief," he said. "The most frightful responsibility . . . would be casting the presidency on me."

Charles J. Guiteau was an unstable man who wanted a government job. After President Garfield repeatedly refused to give him a job, Guiteau shot Garfield in the Washington, D.C., train station.

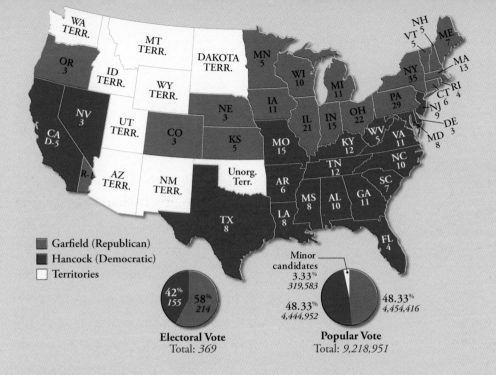

Garfield (Republican)
Hancock (Democratic)
Territories

Electoral Vote
Total: *369*

42% 155 58% 214

Popular Vote
Total: *9,218,951*

Minor candidates
3.33%
319,583

48.33%
4,444,952

48.33%
4,454,416

A DIVIDED NATION

In Arthur's time, just as today, the United States was closely divided politically. James Garfield and Chester Arthur won the White House by a very narrow margin. They won just 8,000 more votes than their opponents out of more than 9 million votes cast. (In the Electoral College, they won more easily, 214 to 155).

Today, the states generally voting Democratic or Republican are divided geographically. The same was true in the mid-to late 1880s. Northern states that had stayed in the Union during the Civil War voted Republican. Southern states voted Democratic. Two swing states helped decide victory in the elections of this era. One was Indiana, where voters rejected big political parties altogether. The other swing state was Arthur's own New York. Though New York had many long-time Republican voters, it was also the home of many new **immigrants** who often voted Democratic. One of the main reasons that the Republicans chose Arthur as their vice presidential candidate was that he was popular with powerful people in New York.

In 1880, both the presidential election and the fight for control of Congress were close. In the House of Representatives, the Republicans won a majority of seats, but the Senate was evenly divided, 37 Republicans and 37 Democrats. Arthur, as vice president, would be responsible for breaking tie votes in the Senate.

President Garfield lingered at death's door for nearly 80 days. On September 19, 1881, he died. The following morning, Arthur took the oath of office from his home in New York City, becoming the 21st president of the United States. He did not make a formal speech, but he did say a few words: "No higher or more assuring proof could exist of the strength and permanence of popular government than the fact that though the chosen of the people be struck down, his . . . successor is peacefully installed without shock or strain." Arthur was talking about President Garfield's death. He reminded Americans that their government was still strong and that it would continue to serve them even if their elected president died.

Arthur was well qualified to be president. After all, he had held important government positions in New York. As a lawyer, he knew the law and the U.S. **Constitution** well. But would Arthur be an honest president? Or would he give jobs to people who cooperated with Conkling and the Stalwarts?

When Garfield was president, Arthur wanted him to give jobs to Conkling's friends and supporters. But as president, Arthur was determined to be a good leader. He wanted to go down in history as an honest and admired man. He tried to follow Garfield's ideals.

As part of his desire to make his own mark, Arthur first set about replacing the rather plain White House

In this cartoon, other politicians look at Arthur, wondering if he will be a good president. Portraits of Andrew Johnson, Millard Fillmore, and John Tyler hang on the wall. All three became president after the death of an elected president, but none were successful in the job. An empty frame awaits Arthur's portrait.

ON THE THRESHOLD OF OFFICE.—WHAT HAVE WE TO EXPECT OF HIM?

Designer Louis Comfort Tiffany created the glass screen for the entrance hall of the White House (seen here on the left). Topaz, ruby, and amethyst jewels were set into the glass.

furnishings with those that were more dignified. The British had attacked and burned the White House during the War of 1812. Ever since then, Americans had considered the White House an important symbol. People believed it should be a source of national pride. Arthur wanted the White House to reflect his sophisticated sense of style. He had many of the simple and ordinary pieces of furniture auctioned off. He fired the kitchen staff, who served bland, tasteless meals, and hired a first-class French chef.

He also hired Louis Comfort Tiffany, an up-and-coming designer whose father had founded Tiffany & Company in New York City. Tiffany's specialty was stained glass. He created colorful, elegant stained-glass lamps and windows and placed them about the White House. Arthur also hired Tiffany to make a stained-glass window to honor his wife, Nell. He had the pane installed in St. John's Church in Washington. From the White House each night, Arthur could see the window lit up by church candles. The memorial to Nell still hangs in the church.

Arthur was an independent president. He tried to work with all members of the Republican Party, not just the Stalwarts. He also worked with members of the other powerful political party, the Democrats. He avoided his old political friends and tried to carry out President Garfield's plans for an honest government.

Arthur continued what Garfield had started in two important ways. First, he completed an investigation of dishonesty within the U.S. Postal Service. Star Routes were private postal routes that brought mail to places that did not receive regular mail service. Some people who ran the routes charged more for the service than they should have. Some even charged for services they did not provide. One of Arthur's political friends played a role in the Star Route **scandal.** Even so, Arthur and his assistants worked to put an end to the dishonesty at the Postal Service.

The second way Arthur tried to carry out Garfield's plans was to support the merit system. He wanted

As a result of the changes Arthur made at the White House, 24 wagonloads of furniture and clothing were sold, including a pair of Abraham Lincoln's pants.

Chester Arthur loved feasts. White House dinners usually included 14 courses and 8 different types of wine.

Robert Todd Lincoln, the son of President Abraham Lincoln, served as secretary of war under presidents Garfield and Arthur.

Because Arthur was a widower, his sister Mary Arthur McElroy served as hostess at White House parties.

people to receive government jobs because of their skills, not because of their loyalty to a party. Many jobs were available in the Treasury Department. At first, Americans were sure Arthur would give most of the positions to Stalwarts. But Arthur appointed Stalwarts to only a few positions.

Starting in 1882, Arthur supported a **bill** called the Pendleton Civil Service Reform Act. Once passed, this new law created the Civil Service Commission, which required that people take tests for many government jobs. The people who scored highest on the tests received the positions. The act also made it illegal for government employees to be required to pay part of their salary to a political party. Many of Arthur's followers turned against him when he signed this act.

The Pendleton Act helped distinguish Arthur as a thoughtful and fair president. For nearly his entire career, he had benefited from the patronage system, which was also called the spoils system. In 1831, a New York senator declared outright, "To the victor belong the spoils." Arthur's fellow Republicans had long practiced this way of thinking. The Pendleton Act was the opposite of the spoils system. It was an unexpected and welcome change.

Grand ceremonies marked the opening of the Brooklyn Bridge in New York City on May 24, 1883. Here, President Arthur leads a group across the bridge as part of the celebration.

On February 21, 1885, President Arthur dedicated the Washington Monument.

Arthur seldom went to bed before two o'clock in the morning.

During Arthur's presidency, there were almost equal numbers of Democrats and Republicans in Congress. It was difficult for Arthur to get bills passed. It seemed as if members of Congress were too busy fighting with each other to make laws that would help the country. Fortunately, the American public approved of the Pendleton Act, so Congress agreed to pass it. Arthur signed the bill into law on January 16, 1883.

SCIENCE AND THE DEATH OF A PRESIDENT

James Garfield (above) lived for more than two months after he was shot. Doctors tried many times to take out the bullet that was lodged in his chest, but they couldn't find it. Two scientists, Simon Newcomb and Alexander Graham Bell, tried to help. Newcomb was working on running electricity through wire coils. He found that when metal was placed near the coils, he could hear a faint hum. He hoped to perfect his invention so that it could be used to locate the bullet.

Bell read about Newcomb in a newspaper. He offered his help, suggesting that his invention, the telephone, might be able to improve Newcomb's invention. It could make the humming sound louder. The two men joined forces and came up with an early version of a metal detector.

On July 26, Bell and Newcomb went to the White House to try their invention. The detector made a humming sound no matter where it was placed on the president's body. Bell and Newcomb left the White House confused and disappointed. Why didn't their invention work?

Bell returned to the lab with Newcomb. They ran more experiments, and their invention worked well. They returned to the White House on the last day of July. The same thing happened again. No matter where they placed the detector on the president's body, they could hear a faint hum.

What was wrong with Bell and Newcomb's invention? The invention wasn't the problem. The problem was the president's bed! It had springs made of metal, so the metal detector kept humming and humming. The White House was one of the few places that had mattresses with metal springs at the time. If Bell and Newcomb had moved the president off the bed and onto the floor, their invention could have found the bullet.

It is still likely that Garfield would have died, however. Doctors had probed for the bullet with dirty hands and instruments. This allowed germs to enter his wounds, causing severe infections.

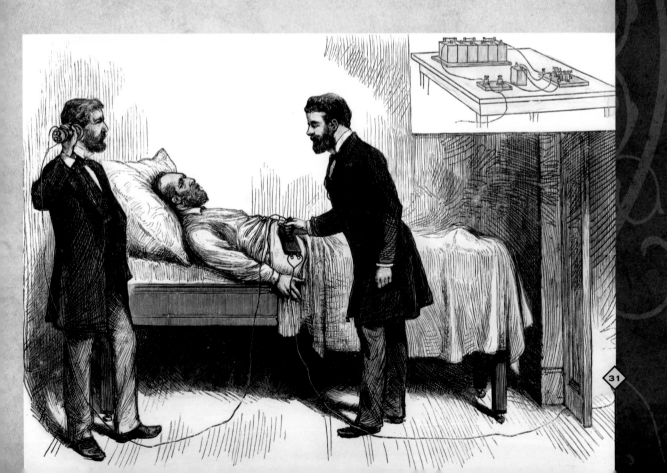

CHAPTER FOUR

A MAN TO RESPECT

Although Chester Arthur did not make campaign promises before taking office, once he found himself president of the United States, he sought to do his best to make the country a better place to live. In speeches before Congress, Arthur encouraged lawmakers to pass laws that would preserve national forests, assist Native Americans, improve funding for public education, and provide medical help for the poor.

White Americans in the West sometimes rioted because they believed that Chinese immigrants were taking their jobs. This illustration shows an attack on Chinese workers in Colorado.

Arthur disagreed with Congress over many issues, including the fate of Chinese immigrants. Some Americans claimed that the Chinese were taking too many jobs, especially in the West. Members of Congress wanted to pass the Chinese Exclusion Act. This law was intended to keep Chinese people from moving to the United States for 20 years. It also would have denied citizenship to U.S. residents of Chinese **ancestry.** Arthur decided

President Chester A. Arthur in a photograph from 1882

to **veto** the bill, for he still believed in civil rights. Congress was determined to pass the bill. Arthur finally signed a different version that limited Chinese immigration for 10 years instead of 20. Unfortunately, it also denied citizenship to Chinese people who had lived in the United States for many years. The act was in force until 1943.

Arthur believed the country needed a stronger military to protect itself against its enemies. He argued that the United States needed to build up its navy. At his urging, Congress agreed to fund the building of 68 new steel ships. This was the beginning of the modern American navy.

Arthur tried to help Native Americans by protecting their lands from settlers who were claiming it as their own. Unfortunately, his efforts failed.

THE FATHER OF THE U.S. NAVY

The U.S. Navy had been among the strongest navies in the world during the Civil War. But by the 1880s, it was one of the weakest. Every major European nation, as well as several Latin American countries, had better navies than the United States. The U.S. Navy was in a poor position to protect the country.

President Arthur decided that the United States needed to rebuild its navy. He had members of his cabinet make suggestions to improve the navy. These ideas became part of the Navy Bill. The main purpose of the bill was to construct 68 new steel ships. At the time, the navy's ships were made of wood.

After a long debate, Congress agreed to the construction of three steel ships. In 1885, before Arthur left office, Congress agreed to build four more. The first four ships that were built were called the ABCD ships because they were named the *Atlanta*, the *Boston*, the *Chicago*, and the *Dolphin*. In the photo above, the *Boston* helps celebrate the 100th anniversary of the U.S. Navy.

The passage of the Navy Bill was a first step toward making the United States a naval power. Arthur also wanted the U.S. Navy to have battleships, but the first of these were not built until the 1890s. He did not have enough support from Congress to achieve his goals. Because of Arthur's efforts, he is sometimes called the "Father of the U.S. Navy."

But more often, Arthur and members of Congress disagreed. Congress proposed a bill to spend $19 million to improve rivers and harbors, especially those in the South. Arthur thought this was a waste of money and vetoed it. Congress overturned his veto, and the bill became law. Even though he lost this fight and several others, Americans respected President Arthur for taking a stand.

Arthur did not gain the support of Congress during his presidency, but he did gain the approval of the American public. Many people who once criticized him were now his supporters. Writer Mark Twain complimented Arthur, saying, "I am but one in 55,000,000; still, in the opinion of this one-fifty-five millionth of the country's population, it would be hard to better President Arthur's **administration.** But don't decide till you hear from the rest."

Arthur owned more than 80 pairs of pants and changed his clothes several times a day.

Some people thought President Arthur spent too much time away from work. This cartoon depicts Arthur (center) and his cabinet asleep when they should be working.

35

Before he died, Chester Arthur had all of his personal papers destroyed. This has left historians with many unanswered questions about his life.

While he was president, Arthur learned that he was suffering from Bright's disease, a kidney disease that did not have a cure. Arthur did not want to tell the American public about his illness for fear that they would lose faith in him. For a while, he thought about running for a second term as president, but he decided against it. In private, he told his son that he simply did not feel well enough to handle the duties of president for four more years.

At the end of Arthur's term as president, he returned to his home in New York. Nearly two years later, on November 18, 1886, he died of Bright's disease.

On November 22, 1886, Arthur was buried next to his wife's grave in Albany, New York. His tomb is topped with a large bronze angel holding a palm branch.

Chester Arthur was known for being elegant and well-dressed.

As president, Chester Arthur proved that he had a mind of his own. He also proved that he did not work for one political party, but for all Americans. Arthur gave the country an honest presidency. He helped rebuild the U.S. Navy. By the end of his term, Arthur had won the respect of American citizens. Alexander McClure, the publisher of the *Philadelphia Times*, once wrote about President Arthur, "No man ever entered the Presidency so profoundly and widely distrusted, and no one ever retired . . . more generally respected."

President Arthur (standing at left) loved fishing. He escaped Washington for fishing trips as often as he could.

Time Line

1821
William and Malvina Arthur, Chester's parents, are married.

1828
William Arthur studies to become a Baptist minister. He becomes the pastor of a church in North Fairfield, Vermont.

1829
Chester Arthur is born on October 5 in North Fairfield.

1835
The Arthurs move to New York State. William Arthur helps start the New York Anti-Slavery Society.

1839
The Arthur family moves to Saratoga County, New York.

1845
Arthur enrolls at Union College in Schenectady, New York.

1848
Arthur graduates from Union College. He begins studying law and working as a schoolteacher.

1851
Arthur becomes the principal of a school in the basement of his father's church in North Pownal, Vermont.

1853
Arthur moves to New York City to work for Erastus D. Culver.

1854
Arthur begins practicing law in New York City.

1855
Arthur defends Elizabeth Jennings, who was forced off a streetcar because she was black. The judge decides that African Americans must be allowed to use public transportation in New York. Arthur also works with Erastus Culver on the Lemmon case, which determines that enslaved people who travel into the state of New York are considered free.

1859
Arthur marries Ellen Lewis Herndon in October.

1860

Arthur campaigns for two Republican candidates: Edwin D. Morgan for governor of New York and Abraham Lincoln for U.S. president. Both candidates win their elections.

1861

The Civil War begins. Arthur is named inspector general and then quartermaster general of New York. His job is to make sure that soldiers have enough food and supplies.

1863

Arthur resigns from his position as quartermaster general. He returns to his law practice and begins a political friendship with Roscoe Conkling, the leader of the Stalwarts.

1865

The Civil War ends.

1868

Arthur and the Stalwarts support General Ulysses S. Grant in the presidential election.

1871

President Ulysses S. Grant appoints Arthur collector of the Port of New York.

1878

President Rutherford B. Hayes fires Arthur from his position at the Port of New York.

1880

Ellen Arthur dies. The Republicans nominate James A. Garfield as their presidential candidate and Arthur as their vice presidential candidate. Garfield and Arthur win the election.

1881

Garfield is sworn in as president on March 4. He is shot on July 2 and dies on September 19. Vice President Arthur becomes the 21st U.S. president.

1882

The Chinese Exclusion Act passes, ending Chinese immigration into the United States for 10 years. Arthur learns that he is suffering from Bright's disease.

1883

Arthur signs the Pendleton Civil Service Reform Act, the nation's first civil service law, which requires people to pass a test to get a government job. It also makes it illegal to require that government employees give part of their salary to a political party.

1884

Congress votes to replace some of the U.S. Navy's wooden ships with steel ones. Arthur gains the nickname "Father of the U.S. Navy." He decides not to run for reelection.

1885

Arthur moves back to New York. He dies on November 18 at age 57.

39

GLOSSARY

administration (ad-min-uh-STRAY-shun)
An administration is the period of time that a president holds office. Arthur did not gain the support of Congress during his administration.

ancestry (AN-sess-tree) A person's ancestry is his or her family line. The Chinese Exclusion Act denied citizenship to people of Chinese ancestry.

appointed (uh-POYN-ted) If someone is appointed to a position, he or she is asked by an important official to accept the position. President Grant appointed Arthur collector of the Port of New York.

bill (BILL) A bill is an idea for a new law that is presented to a group of lawmakers. Arthur supported a bill called the Pendleton Civil Service Reform Act.

cabinet (KAB-nit) A cabinet is the group of people who advise a president. Members of Arthur's cabinet made suggestions to improve the navy.

campaign (kam-PAYN) A campaign is the process of running for an election, including activities such as giving speeches or attending rallies. Arthur worked on the campaigns of Republican candidates.

candidate (KAN-duh-dayt) A candidate is a person running in an election. Arthur campaigned for the first Republican candidate for president, John Frémont.

civil rights (SIV-ul RITES) Civil rights are basic rights that are guaranteed to all citizens under the U.S. Constitution. As a lawyer, Arthur protected the civil rights of African Americans.

compromise (KOM-pruh-myz) A compromise is a way to settle a disagreement in which both sides give up part of what they want. President Garfield tried to reach a compromise with Senator Conkling over government jobs.

constitution (kon-stih-TOO-shun) A constitution is the set of basic principles that govern a state, country, or society. As a lawyer, Arthur knew the U.S. Constitution well.

convention (kun-VEN-shun) A convention is a meeting. Political parties hold national conventions every four years to choose their presidential candidates.

customs (KUS-tumz) Customs are fees or taxes charged on imports or exports. Arthur was in charge of collecting customs for the port of New York.

debate (di-BAYT) A debate is a competition in which people discuss a question or topic, considering reasons for and against it. Arthur belonged to the debate club at Union College.

faction (FAK-shun) A faction is a smaller group within a bigger organization, such as a political party. Factions often disagree with other members of the larger organization.

federal (FED-uh-rul) Federal means having to do with the central government of the United States, rather than a state or city government. Republicans controlled the federal government after the Civil War.

immigrants (IM-uh-grunts) Immigrants are people who have moved to a new country to live. The Chinese Exclusion Act kept Chinese immigrants from becoming citizens for 10 years.

nominated (NOM-uh-nayt-ed) If a political party nominated someone, it chose him or her to run for a political office. In 1880, the Republicans nominated James Garfield as their presidential candidate.

pneumonia (nuh-MOHN-yuh) Pneumonia is a disease of the lungs. Ellen Arthur died of pneumonia.

political party (puh-LIT-uh-kul PAR-tee) A political party is a group of people who share similar ideas about how to run a government. Arthur belonged to the Republican political party.

politics (PAWL-uh-tiks) Politics refers to the actions and practices of the government. Arthur's interest in politics allowed him to share his antislavery beliefs with others.

quartermaster (KWOR-tur-mas-tur) A quartermaster is an army officer who provides clothing and other goods for troops. Arthur served as a quartermaster during the Civil War.

salary (SAL-uh-ree) A salary is money a person is paid regularly for work. The Pendleton Act made it illegal to require workers to pay part of their salary to a political party.

scandal (SKAN-dul) A scandal is a shameful action that shocks the public. Arthur continued Garfield's investigation of the Star Route scandal.

territories (TAYR-uh-tor-eez) Territories are lands or regions, especially lands that belong to a government. Republicans were against the spread of slavery to new territories.

Union (YOON-yen) The Union is another name for the United States of America. During the Civil War, the North was called the Union.

veto (VEE-toh) A veto is the president's power to refuse to sign a bill into law. Arthur vetoed a bill to improve rivers and harbors.

THE UNITED STATES GOVERNMENT

The United States government is divided into three equal branches: the executive, the legislative, and the judicial. This division helps prevent abuses of power because each branch has to answer to the other two. No one branch can become too powerful.

EXECUTIVE BRANCH

PRESIDENT
VICE PRESIDENT
DEPARTMENTS

The job of the executive branch is to enforce the laws. It is headed by the president, who serves as the spokesperson for the United States around the world. The president signs bills into law and appoints important officials such as federal judges. He or she is also the commander in chief of the U.S. military. The president is assisted by the vice president, who takes over if the president dies or cannot carry out the duties of the office.

The executive branch also includes various departments, each focused on a specific topic. They include the Defense Department, the Justice Department, and the Agriculture Department. The department heads, along with other officials such as the vice president, serve as the president's closest advisers, called the cabinet.

LEGISLATIVE BRANCH

CONGRESS
Senate and
House of Representatives

The job of the legislative branch is to make the laws. It consists of Congress, which is divided into two parts: the Senate and the House of Representatives. The Senate has 100 members, and the House of Representatives has 435 members. Each state has two senators. The number of representatives a state has varies depending on the state's population.

Besides making laws, Congress also passes budgets and enacts taxes. In addition, it is responsible for declaring war, maintaining the military, and regulating trade with other countries.

JUDICIAL BRANCH

SUPREME COURT
COURTS OF APPEALS
DISTRICT COURTS

The job of the judicial branch is to interpret the laws. It consists of the nation's federal courts. Trials are held in district courts. During trials, judges must decide what laws mean and how they apply. Courts of appeals review the decisions made in district courts.

The nation's highest court is the Supreme Court. If someone disagrees with a court of appeals ruling, he or she can ask the Supreme Court to review it. The Supreme Court may refuse. The Supreme Court makes sure that decisions and laws do not violate the Constitution.

CHOOSING
THE PRESIDENT

It may seem odd, but American voters don't elect the president directly. Instead, the president is chosen using what is called the Electoral College.

Each state gets as many votes in the Electoral College as its combined total of senators and representatives in Congress. For example, Iowa has two senators and five representatives, so it gets seven electoral votes. Although the District of Columbia does not have any voting members in Congress, it gets three electoral votes. Usually, the candidate who wins the most votes in any given state receives all of that state's electoral votes.

To become president, a candidate must get more than half of the Electoral College votes. There are a total of 538 votes in the Electoral College, so a candidate needs 270 votes to win. If nobody receives 270 Electoral College votes, the House of Representatives chooses the president.

With the Electoral College system, the person who receives the most votes nationwide does not always receive the most electoral votes. This happened most recently in 2000, when Al Gore received half a million more national votes than George W. Bush. Bush became president because he had more Electoral College votes.

THE WHITE HOUSE

The White House is the official home of the president of the United States. It is located at 1600 Pennsylvania Avenue NW in Washington, D.C. In 1792, a contest was held to select the architect who would design the president's home. James Hoban won. Construction took eight years.

The first president, George Washington, never lived in the White House. The second president, John Adams, moved into the house in 1800, though the inside was not yet complete. During the War of 1812, British soldiers burned down much of the White House. It was rebuilt several years later.

The White House was changed through the years. Porches were added, and President Theodore Roosevelt added the West Wing. President William Taft changed the shape of the presidential office, making it into the famous Oval Office. While Harry Truman was president, the old house was discovered to be structurally weak. All the walls were reinforced with steel, and the rooms were rebuilt.

Today, the White House has 132 rooms (including 35 bathrooms), 28 fireplaces, and 3 elevators. It takes 570 gallons of paint to cover the outside of the six-story building. The White House provides the president with many ways to relax. It includes a putting green, a jogging track, a swimming pool, a tennis court, and beautifully landscaped gardens. The White House also has a movie theater, a billiard room, and a one-lane bowling alley.

PRESIDENTIAL PERKS

The job of president of the United States is challenging. It is probably one of the most stressful jobs in the world. Because of this, presidents are paid well, though not nearly as well as the leaders of large corporations. In 2007, the president earned $400,000 a year. Presidents also receive extra benefits that make the demanding job a little more appealing.

★ **Camp David:** In the 1940s, President Franklin D. Roosevelt chose this heavily wooded spot in the mountains of Maryland to be the presidential retreat, where presidents can relax. Even though it is a retreat, world business is conducted there. Most famously, President Jimmy Carter met with Middle Eastern leaders at Camp David in 1978. The result was a peace agreement between Israel and Egypt.

★ *Air Force One*: The president flies on a jet called *Air Force One*. It is a Boeing 747-200B that has been modified to meet the president's needs.

Air Force One is the size of a large home. It is equipped with a dining room, sleeping quarters, a conference room, and office space. It also has two kitchens that can provide food for up to 50 people.

★ **The Secret Service:** While not the most glamorous of the president's perks, the Secret Service is one of the most important. The Secret Service is a group of highly trained agents who protect the president and the president's family.

★ **The Presidential State Car:** The presidential limousine is a stretch Cadillac DTS.

It has been armored to protect the president in case of attack. Inside the plush car are a foldaway desk, an entertainment center, and a communications console.

★ **The Food:** The White House has five chefs who will make any food the president wants. The White House also has an extensive wine collection.

★ **Retirement:** A former president receives a pension, or retirement pay, of just under $180,000 a year. Former presidents also receive Secret Service protection for the rest of their lives.

FACTS

QUALIFICATIONS

To run for president, a candidate must

- ★ be at least 35 years old
- ★ be a citizen who was born in the United States
- ★ have lived in the United States for 14 years

TERM OF OFFICE

A president's term of office is four years.
No president can stay in office for more than two terms.

ELECTION DATE

The presidential election takes place every four years on the first Tuesday of November.

INAUGURATION DATE

Presidents are inaugurated on January 20.

OATH OF OFFICE

I do solemnly swear I will faithfully execute the office of the President of the United States and will to the best of my ability preserve, protect, and defend the Constitution of the United States.

WRITE A LETTER TO THE PRESIDENT

One of the best things about being a U.S. citizen is that Americans get to participate in their government. They can speak out if they feel government leaders aren't doing their jobs. They can also praise leaders who are going the extra mile. Do you have something you'd like the president to do? Should the president worry more about the environment and encourage people to recycle? Should the government spend more money on our schools? You can write a letter to the president to say how you feel!

1600 Pennsylvania Avenue
Washington, D.C. 20500
You can even send an e-mail to: president@whitehouse.gov

BOOKS

Elish, Dan. *Chester A. Arthur: America's 21st President.* New York: Children's Press, 2004.

Feldman, Ruth Tenzer. *Chester A. Arthur.* Minneapolis: Twenty-First Century Books, 2007.

Francis, Sandra. *Rutherford B. Hayes.* Mankato, MN: The Child's World, 2009.

Rubel, David. *Scholastic Encyclopedia of the Presidents and Their Times.* New York: Scholastic, 2005.

Santella, Andrew. *Chester A. Arthur.* Minneapolis: Compass Point Books, 2004.

VIDEOS

The History Channel Presents The Presidents. DVD (New York: A&E Home Video, 2005).

National Geographic's Inside the White House. DVD (Washington, DC: National Geographic Video, 2003).

INTERNET SITES

Visit our Web page for lots of links about Chester A. Arthur and other U.S. presidents:

http://www.childsworld.com/links

Note to Parents, Teachers, and Librarians: We routinely verify our Web links to make sure they are safe, active sites—so encourage your readers to check them out!

INDEX

ABCD ships, 34
abolitionists, 5, 7, 11, 38
African Americans, rights of, 7–8, 38
Anti-Nebraska Convention, 6–7, 39
Arthur, Chester
  birth of, 4, 38
  campaigning work, 8, 9, 12, 39
  as customs collector, 15–17, 19, 39
  death of, 36, 39
  education of, 5–6, 38
  honesty of, 25, 27, 37
  illness of, 36, 39
  law practice, 7–8, 10, 38, 39
  marriage of, 11, 38
  navy, rebuilding of, 33–34, 37, 39
  as president, 24–29, 32–37, 39
  public opinion of, 35, 37
  as quartermaster general, 12, 13–14, 39
  veto power, 35
  as vice president, 21–22, 39
  as vice-presidential candidate, 17–18, 20, 23, 39
Arthur, Chester Alan Jr., 11
Arthur, Ellen (daughter), 11
Arthur, Ellen (wife), 10–11, 12, 18, 27, 38, 39
Arthur, Malvina, 4–5, 38
Arthur, William, 4–5, 38

Bell, Alexander Graham, 30–31
Bovay, Alan Earl, 9
Bright's disease, 36, 39
Brooklyn Bridge, 29

Chinese Exclusion Act, 33, 39
civil rights, 7–8, 33, 38
Civil Service Commission, 28
Civil War, 12, 13, 23, 34, 39
Conkling, Roscoe, 14, 16, 17–18, 21–22, 25, 39
Culver, Erastus D., 10–12, 38

Democratic Party, 9, 20, 23, 29
Democratic-Republican Party, 9

Frémont, John C., 8, 9

Gardiner, Henry D., 10
Garfield, James, 8, 17–18, 21–22, 25, 39
Grant, Ulysses S., 14–15, 39
Guiteau, Charles J., 22

Hayes, Rutherford B., 16–17, 19, 22, 39
Herndon, Dabney, 12
Herndon, Ellen. See Arthur, Ellen (wife)

immigration, 33

Jefferson, Thomas, 9
Jennings, Elizabeth, 7, 38

Kansas-Nebraska Act, 6–7, 10

Lemmon, Jonathan, 8, 38
Lincoln, Abraham, 9, 12, 13, 22, 28, 39
Lincoln, Robert T., 28

McClure, Alexander, 37
McElroy, Mary Arthur, 28
merit system, 19, 28–29
Morgan, Edwin D., 12, 13, 39

Native Americans, 33
Navy Bill, 34
New York Anti-Slavery Society, 4, 38
New York Customs House, 15, 19
Newcomb, Simon, 30–31

Paine, Elijah, 8
patronage, 15–17, 19, 21–22
Pendleton Civil Service Reform Act, 28, 29, 39

Republican Party, 8, 9, 14–15, 16–19, 20, 21–22, 23, 27, 29, 39

Seymour, Horatio, 14
slavery, 5, 6–8, 9, 11, 12
Stalwarts, 14–15, 19, 21–22, 25, 27, 28, 39
Star Route scandal, 27
Stone, Malvina. See Arthur, Malvina

Tiffany, Louis Comfort, 26, 27
Twain, Mark, 35

Union College, 5–6, 38
U.S. Navy, 33–34, 37, 39
U.S. Postal Service scandal, 27

War of 1812, 26
Whig Party, 9
White House, 25–27, 30–31